Books by John Hollander

Poetry

Blue Wine and Other Poems   1979
Spectral Emanations: New and Selected Poems   1978
Reflections on Espionage   1976
Tales Told of the Fathers   1975
The Head of the Bed   1974
Town and Country Matters   1972
The Night Mirror   1971
Types of Shape   1969
Visions from the Ramble   1965
Movie-Going   1962
A Crackling of Thorns   1958

Criticism

Vision and Resonance   1975
        Two Senses of Poetic Form
The Untuning of the Sky   1961
        Ideas of Music in English Poetry 1500–1700

For Children

The Immense Parade on Supererogation Day
        and What Happened to It   1972
The Quest of the Gole   1966

THE NIGHT MIRROR

THE NIGHT MIRROR

POEMS BY

JOHN HOLLANDER

ATHENEUM   NEW YORK

1979

The poems in this book first appeared in a number of periodicals, and I acknowledge their permission to reprint as follows:

POETRY: *Another Firefly; As the Sparks Fly Upward; The Curse; Hall of Ocean Life; Kinds of Kindling; The Long and the Short of It; Sunday A.M. Not in Manhattan; String Player in the Shack; Two Slices of Sequoia.*

THE NEW YORKER: *Alaska Brown Bear; His Master's Voice; Munich Showdown; The Night Mirror; White Noise.*

PARTISAN REVIEW: *The Antiquities in Room 101; Evening Wolves.*

HARPER'S MAGAZINE: *Letter to Borges; Music Volute.*

SOUTHERN REVIEW: *Damoetas; In Fog, Tacit, Outside Cherbourg.*

NEW AMERICAN REVIEW: *Adam's Task; What I See When I Look Up.*

THE LISTENER: *Crossing a Bare Common; Drat the Cat.*

COLUMBIA FORUM: *Ad Musam; Under Capricorn.*

MODERN OCCASIONS: *Power Failure.*

YALE REVIEW: *To Richard Howard On Our Birthdays.*

TRIQUARTERLY: *Poem of Pooballs.*

THE NEW STATESMAN: *Under Cancer.*

AMERICAN JUDAISM: *At the New Year.*

NEW YORK QUARTERLY: *The Poem of One Line.*

PEBBLE: *Sent on a Sheet of Paper*, etc.

ARMADILLO: *The Moon at Noon.*

LAST DITCH: *White Above Green.*

NEW YORK TIMES: *Stooping for Salad* © 1971 by The New York Times Co. Reprinted by permission.

The Will, The Bird and *I Am* were specially translated for Irving Howe and Eliezer Greenberg's TREASURY OF MODERN YIDDISH POETRY.

AD BUNNAM

Golden pears hanging
Over full, wild roses;
The land in the lake.

Behold the far swans,
Drunk with the images
They kiss, bills dunking

Into dark water.
What pictures shall we drink
In the midland cold?

Summer's shadow lies
As if unpromised, dry
Along silent walls;

Windward we sit, watched
From behind pennants that
Slap the windy air.

CONTENTS

PART I   THE NIGHT MIRROR

PART II   ANNIVERSARIES

I

THE NIGHT MIRROR

UNDER CANCER

On the Memorial building's
Terrace the sun has been buzzing
Unbearably, all the while
The white baking happens
To the shadow of the table's
White-painted iron. It darkens,
Meaning that the sun is stronger,
That I am invisibly darkening
Too, the while I whiten.
And only after the stretching
And getting up, still sweating,
My shirt striped like an awning
Drawn on over airlessness;
After the cool shades
(As if of a long arcade
Where footsteps echo gravely)
Have devoured the light;
Only after the cold of
Plunge and shower, the pale
Scent of deodorant stick
Smelling like gin and limes,
And another stripy shirt
Can come, homing in at last,
The buzzing of having been burnt.
Only then, intimations
Of tossing, hot in the dark
Night, where all the long while
Silently, along edges,
There is flaking away.

In this short while of light
My shadow darkens without
Lengthening ever, ever.

Frozen stubble, bone
Of the summer's cornfield, stretches
Away from the concrete belt
The road tightens against
The earth's chest. It is dry
And unbelievably cold.
They are hot, though, each
For the heat of the other: their car,
Maddened by visibilities,
Scours across the country:
Their hands, trembling with touch,
Pause for a time in cloth
But a time too long. There is no
Cover for them or their car——
Curving hummock nor bare
Slumbering lap of hollow——
To contain them while their white
And chattering flesh becomes
Enclosed in its own cells
Lest perhaps the thick and
Warming tears of love
They weep into each other
Manage to bind them up
In the company of joy;
Lest, like weather and earth
Sprung into green, he spring
Inside of her to hide
His wise head in her cave
Of promises that beyond
Winter there shall come
Bright, hot moments yet.

But crowded away in their car
From the unwarming light
By which wide fields and sky
Reflect each other's emptiness,
Their bodies, sobbing at last,
Would be reclaimed by winter.

They know such weather well.
Still, unnaturally eager,
They fly on over the bony
Road, looking out (out, never
In at each other) for somewhere
Else, for somewhere other
Than the unfailing brightness
Of these dumb, hopeful fields
Whose tongues will unlock only
In the uninventive course
Of season (like a sick
Joke about fulfillment)
Finally succeeding season.

WHITE ABOVE GREEN

High on this whitest place,
Towering into the wild,
Green wind in which we turn,
Our eyes burn. Your face
Is a wide mind——my own——
With mild hair blown
Over the sky your eyes
Turn to, while mine trace
Descents of towers lower
Than ours: plunged, yearning
For shaded lawns (those mild
Green minds no winds burn)
Turning slowly below
The blowing on our windy heights.

Minds are whitened, our hands
Grown even now in green
Confusions among wild,
Shaded places: as if sand
From a wide, far, white beach
Lying like a felled tower
Among green dunes, blowing
Into our widening eyes
Burned not at all, but turned
Our tongues to grass, our minds
To fiery, white unknowns
While our wide hearts, our whirling
Hearts, confused, were burning.

Wide, wide are the high places!

High on our tower
Where the winds were
Did my head turning
Turn yours,
Or were we burning
In the one wind?

Our wide stares pinned
To a spinning world,
We burned; my head,
Turning to yours
On that white tower,
Whirled high in fire.

All heights are our
Towers of desire;
All shaded spaces
Our valleys, enclosing
Now darkening places
Of unequal repose.

How tower-high were
Our whitest places
Where my head widely
Turned into yours
In the spaces of spinning,
In burning wind!

*How dark and far
Apart valleys are . . .*

THE CURSE

Outside, a delicate arch
Of steel rises above
The desolate streets, and westward,
The river's long-since-fallen
Water lies darkly quiet,
Holding in its broad lap
Golden lights from rewarding
Shores, showered in payment;
Slowly the moon-tied flow tugs
Downward; everything runs
Unstopped out of the bay.

Inside, the yellow lights
Of the hopeless IRT
Die for a second, as car
By car, the train blacks out,
Moment echoing moment.
They stand at the front window
Watching the opening tunnel
That crashes into their faces.
She is a week late.
They are waiting to stop waiting
For something inside to happen.

On the surface of it,
A blessing will come in time,
Falling on her one morning
When they are separate;
When they meet that evening
She will tell him sweetly,
On the wide street, in the spill
Of fluorescence from the grocer's:
"It's all right now." "I thought so."
Blessed in the change, they scamper
Uptown toward a shining corner.

Blessed? Cursed? or merely
Commanded to be? To issue
Forth from love's subway
Is to reclaim a world
Not lost, but checked at an entrance:
Their fear's sole issue only
The delayed mundane omen,
They move from depth to surface,
Over the skin-deep avenues
Then, along and across them.
And so on. And so forth.

But, at bottom, that light
Will again be revoked.
As when the moon's dark falls
Across the tar of rooftops,
Gathering the pale shadows
Of a fortnight past,
There in the wheal and flare
Of another underground
Tube, the shadows of coming
Shadows mold their cheeks,
Their bright, unhollowed eyes.

"CROSSING A BARE COMMON, IN SNOW PUDDLES, AT TWILIGHT, UNDER A CLOUDED SKY"

There is no lamppost, here
Half the way across.

I have been coming toward
What, in that dull spilling
Of light from behind houses
Will have been abandoned
By the time I have passed
Over toward rimming trees. . . .

By the time? Abandoned.
Not by the moment of knowing
How far I have yet come?
No. *By my darkening back*
Becoming what will be? No.

The accessible horizon
Into which tall shapes sink
Accepts all walking forms
As if through final portals.
I am not hurrying there;
Long door-shadows extended
Toward me seem undeserved.

Why here? Why now, then? Why
I? Everywhere around
Flattening instances fade
Into the ground,
That is to say, the sky.

Not blacked-out, but wrapped in a clear
Blackening air, the avenues
Lead only into night, and we,
Inspectors of shadow, waving
Our wands of watery flashlight
Up at the unresponsive stone
Of high apartment buildings, must
Seem abandoned air-raid wardens,
Crawling like slow, dark bugs from a
Quarter-century's hiding to
Assert some eminent domain.
Like a dead boy and girl we walk
August sidewalks, still hot in this
Blend of real and artificial
Night——a girl and boy killed six months
Before, just past the Laurel Hill
Tunnel on the Pennsylvania
Turnpike, say, as unshining ice
Declared itself too late, in one
Black, spinning mirroring of stars
Which, as they were realized as
Stars, blackened. And as if we were
Come back to walk around the block
Where our parents' apartment was,
We turn the corner, westward, not
Quite thirty; a spirit, our small
Baby seven storeys up, breathes,
Snorts, rasps and gurgles in the black
Silence of unconditioned air.

Our steps have no weight. In the west
Across the park, the lights wink on
In windows that suddenly pierce
Cut-out forms throbbing in and out
Of vision against a curtain
Of ruined sunset. Here in our
Valleys, there is no moon; nor will
Our barely-clasped hands ever be
Lit by more than the pale glow of
This knowledge, of our ghostly touch.

THE NIGHT MIRROR

What it showed was always the same——
A vertical panel with him in it,
Being a horrible bit of movement
At the edge of knowledge, overhanging
The canyons of nightmare. And when the last
Glimpse was enough——his grandmother,
Say, with a blood-red face, rising
From her Windsor chair in the warm lamplight
To tell him something——he would scramble up,
Waiting to hear himself shrieking, and gain
The ledge of the world, his bed, lit by
The pale rectangle of window, eclipsed
By a dark shape, but a shape that moved
And saw and knew and mistook its reflection
In the tall panel on the closet door
For itself. The silver corona of moonlight
That gloried his glimpsed head was enough
To send him back into silences (choosing
Fear in those chasms below), to reject
Freedom of wakeful seeing, believing
And feeling, for peace and the bondage to horrors
Welling up only from deep within
That dark planet head, spinning beyond
The rim of the night mirror's range, huge
And cold, on the pillow's dark side.

II

ANNIVERSARIES

MORS

From the French of Victor Hugo

I saw that reaper. In her field she strode,
Reaping and harvesting all that she mowed,
Black skeleton, letting the twilight pass——
All tremble at its shadow in the grass;
Man kept the glimmering of the scythe in sight.
Under triumphant arches, triumphers quite
Tumbled; in desert Babylon alone
Throne she turned scaffold, scaffold into throne;
Gold into dust; and children into birds;
Mothers' eyes, rivers; roses into turds.
"Give back this little being," women cried,
"Why was it made to live, just to have died?"
Only one sob rang out through all the lands,
Black pallets put forth bony-fingered hands;
A chill wind rustled through unnumbered shrouds;
Under the dismal scythe, bewildered crowds
Resembled shivering herds in shadowed flight:
Under their mournful feet, terror and night.
Behind her, his forehead bathed in gentle flame,
With souls in sheaves, a smiling angel came.

17

DAMOETAS

In memory of Andrew Chiappe,
teacher of Shakespeare, dead in France
May, 1967.

In memory of Andrew Chiappe,
teacher of Shakespeare, dead in France
May, 1967.

1

The birth of a middle year
Lies not in the buried tube of pinched
First months, but later in the clear
Leap into green being. Spring
Has delivered a new age now, and death
Shall flash into flower on every hedge,
For it is a gray
May: we have reached the edge
Of one more stream to be crossed
One way only into these broad,
Lean fields of grief, all speech lost
In buzzing, unmown silences,
Thick with the ticking of countless watches.
And in our middle, listening time
We hear each death
As the hard echo of our breath
And read the shapes of sorrow in
The shadows of the smothering, high
Cumulus that scud across
The bottom of an unwatched sky,
Yielding no sobs of rain.

Our teachers have started leaving.
Our fields are darkening, and late
Flies wind an autumnal horn
As we pause at the unlatched gate;
But it is grief alone
That leads us to loitering among the fictions:
Distractions of fields by water,
Thoughts of memorial stone,
Wide courts, triumphant swans, and pale reflections.

2

This was too heavy a spring, the April
Vacant, the conditional May
Shattered with cold, and now old
Damoetas dead: and suddenly thereby
Our dying has commenced, and dry
Languages of mourning hold
Fast in their unfilled beds,
Stony and motionless, used up. And
Praise? It frays in our sharpened,
Shiny, ironic machines. And Plaint?
It will water nothing that has really dried.
And Explaining who a teacher was
Is wearyingly like
Expounding unopened volumes of self
Aloud to a dusty, silent hall
Dim with disbelief, in a late
Afternoon at the end of fall.

Damoetas dead: back from treading
Some of his own youthful fields, I see
Some white sheet bleaching on the edge
Of hay piled up and distant trees; I see
As through the green spikes and hidden white
Of the distant-flowered sedge,
Down an oracular canal;
The noblest and the brassiest
Impresa of gawkiness redeemed,
And beauty whose terminal
Is eloquence, floats on the gleaming
Water. Swans, though, do not sing at last;
Posthumous, unlocked pages shred
In eager fingers; and the dead,
Still in their silent past,
Gowned in remembrances, the dons undone
Stroll on their long lawns across
The narrow river from us.

Now noon. And evening soon; but stand
Here, for a space, with death ascendant
On the green bank, a low bridge on each hand,
With dropped eyes, O annual, grand
Tourist: Watch all the arch, old emblems fall
Into a processional
Sequence of watery reflections
Under an intermittent sun,
And then go westward home,
Lest the learned gestures,
Laughing and dancing on a shaded lawn,
Draw you back with a caress
Toward shallow deeps
And suddenly empty pastures
Along that dreaming stream, which keeps
Only the shadows that will soon be gone.

3

Echoes of all elegies
Sounded what I had to say
As my breath was sucked away
When the winds rose on the seas.

I remembered breathlessness
In a warm and windless room,
Windowing November gloom,
Bright with his attentiveness.

White hands darted in the air;
Meanings, seized like fireflies
Flashing in our summer skies,
Fell on green minds everywhere.

Ancient cadences return:
Meadows of the gray concrete
Soft beneath our rapid feet
Echo as within an urn;

Lowing trolley-cars once more
Clatter homeward, while nearby
Fiery sirens tear the sky
From the city's threshing-floor.

Evening constellations; pied
Neon clouds among their gold;
Flocks of hope head for a fold
High in sweet, bleak Morningside.

Sunsets drop behind the park
Where the wide, wide river runs;
Wondering boys, whose eyes like suns,
Dazzle as they face the dark—

Mustapha and Portugal
Bobby and Farouk, struck by
That wide, unattending eye,
Aimed beyond the visual,

Hoping to discern a brief
Round significance some night,
Catch it up, and pluck a bright
Global dewdrop from a leaf.

Brightness rises from the burned:
Phoenix and the firefly
Flame eternally, and die
Only while the page is turned.

4

Now summer slips away
Between green banks: water,
Swans and distances under a curving dark
Of stone bridge lingering around a bend,
As high, bright noon goes gray and dull
And cancelled shadows
Of our movement over meadows
Only appear lingering for a while
Among other reflections
Before the late and future rain.

But high in summer, even,
Beyond this old, narrow park,
Full in the shining day,
What could Shadow have to say
To Sunlight, about the dark
Massiveness of substance
Intervening, as an opaque
Parent come between the shade
And its radiant creator?
Shadows keep their silences
In life as in death later:
As in water, lain on meadow.

Past lawn, on meadow, we have been
Walking by water, in the chill
Of afternoon, remembering stone,
Then startled by pale orchid stars
Thrust upward through a thickening green
Of autumn grass: the meadow saffron,
Ghost of the crocus, haunting fields
Of dalliance that will yet
In the green winter, blear and wet,
Remain like ripe, ungathered grain.

Meanwhile across the broadest water
A land away westward, home, the pale
Golden grass and the dun
Bones of the grass lie dismembered,
Unquickened in the dumbly wintering sun.

Laughing thorns crackled beneath my kettle: would
They had been able to flame against the dark
    Gray, cold sky of a mountain morning,
        Mist overhanging the quickened ground;

Trembling with early excitement, chilled, I felt
Darkness in part of my back the earth still kept
    Touching, watching the rising sunlight's
        Pure, silent burning among the leaves.

Laurel burns snappily too, as if the same
Fires that gnaw at the fronds of green renown
    Cackled over a foolish branch of
        Bay crashing, verdant, against my brow.

Not having disembarked,
Shades among shades, we wait until
The gentle, insistent tender nears
To bear some of our shades away.
Harboring arms accept. It disappears.

Away we turn, awakening
A long memorial turbulence.

Stretching ahead from the after-rail,
This wash, this prophecy,
Leads the eye out of vision, where I see
Even now, the moon's broad track
Golden and treacherous, along
Wide swells, extending toward its source
But leading only into black,
Lost waters, like lunacies of hope
At night. But now the fast
Projections of high clouds have wiped
That frightful trail into grisaille,
Leaving the following eye
Safe with its mere desolations
Of endlessly broken water.

Ahead, decks tremble; unheard below
Hearts, turbines roar.
Cutting through what waters remain
Between us and an ultimate shore,
We sink into our corpulence.
Bunches of self gaze past railings,
Whose sorrowing, stern glance reveals
Nothing: for what does the sea
Yield up to hungering sight? The shining seals
Nosing toward distant light? or gay
Porpoises that leap
Against a far, bright sky
For instants, beyond their element?
Or a gray wake, thirty spaces wide
Across a page, a tide
Of wash, leading and following
The eye into unminding error?

What legacies of our voyages?
What shadows sunk beneath the broken mirror?

SENT ON A SHEET OF PAPER WITH A HEART SHAPE CUT OUT OF THE MIDDLE OF IT

Empty, or open-hearted? Where
A full heart spoke once, now a strong
Outline is the most I dare:
A window opening onto fair
Shining meadows of hopefullness? Or long
Silence where there once was song,
Waves of remembrance in the darkening air.

TO RICHARD HOWARD ON OUR BIRTHDAYS

"et quand l'Hippogriffe a relayé Pégase"

Shedding the scales of early
October's sign where your
Moment is counterpoised,
The emerging scorpion raises
His blazoned tail and poisoned
Sting, as in amazement——
Mirror of mine that, surely,
You must be feeling too,

At where we've got to, and what
It all seems to have come to:
Our fortieth year to earth.
October glows, those embers
On either side, and dumb
Winds brush across gray water,
Red flakes fall to the hearthrug.
We're water that remembers,

Our surfaces reflecting,
Our deeps submerged in dream,
Veined with currents that falter,
Moments that chill and quicken:
Too young yet to expect
Poison from standing water,
Once we gazed at a gleaming
Quarry pool, where a sickening

Pond lay, thick with growths,
Just over the rock we stood on,
Giggling at such an emblem;
While Cal was splashing madly
In the bright, spring-fed good one,
Echoes rose and scattered,
All the bad pool's floating
Gardens of garbage trembled.

We took to the clear water,
Writing our names in the brooks
We hoped were spring-fed too.
Now, standing by a lake
Ringed with mountains, our backs
Presented to the viewer,
We wait for a star to break
Out of the twilight of autumn.

What kind of a late-riser
Hanging over their landscape
Will our cloaked, hatted figures
Be vouchsafed? The Great Bell,
With twelve bright stars? The Hand
Of Orpheus? The Shell?
Some older sign, disguised
As our own asterism?

As the flaring Hippogriff
Pale Pegasus gave way to
Himself fades out behind us
Like mad old ways of reading
Appearances, see, it brightens!
——Off in an ever-shifting
Of its direction we lay to
The dazzle of its speed—

There! the ascending New One,
Throwing off the rummage
Of shadows it was bred in.
It leaps up toward the bound
Of the great, blue eye we're hidden
Under and wedded to,
Astonishing even its image,
Outspeeding its own sound.

AD MUSAM

O my Dear,
I have been getting it all
Wrong about us for so
Many a year;

I have presented you
With all that I thought I had
To give: small boxes; my water
Colors of blue

Ocean; some truer
Photographs of pitch darkness
I let expose through the night;
Blue beads, and bluer

Papery flowers
I bought in a bad boutique
On a somewhat dangerous street,
Long after hours;

Meals I have made
You——soups that brooded for weeks,
Blossom pies; curried rememberings and
Mauve lemonade;

Pawn tickets (two),
One for a bright, green object
Whose shape I forget, and one for a
Picture of you;

My winnings at cards
That summer I only won
One game; my nautilus shell;
Several yards

Of peacock and gold
Brocade; my many-stringed
Archlute; half of my ice-cream,
Sweet and still cold, . . .

I gave. I recall.
Drop by corrosive drop,
Through these holes in my memory
Ah, how they fall

Gifts that seemed the measure
Of giving: I wished to withhold
Nothing, but thought to spare you the
Trash.——Or the Treasure

Perhaps? As I cross
The graying December park in
A wind that shrieks and sunders,
Doubled with loss

And straightforward motion,
I approach the evening of Autumn
And stumble on something sunk in the
Sheep-Meadow's ocean,

Something like mud,
That shone once, now turned to what
Reads, by this vast, dim lamp as the
Color of blood.

Love, love, take
This lost blob I'd keep not
For my own, or for other alms, or for
Keeping's sake,

But had only hid
For unknowing of worth, for want
Of age, for mistaking yours.
Now I am rid

Of present giving:
This is our season, Bright Sister.
We are both of an age; I'll not spend it
Loving, but living

Your life, and you, mine.
Now! Snowflakes! as if inside
The cold of the whole dark globe, the
Fire of nine

Fictions were flinging
Light; as if frozen sparks
Leap downward as they surround me,
Dancing and singing.

DRAT THE CAT

The bad kitten at the bottom of my house has never read
   Through the Looking-Glass
But some kind of dream has just stopped now, and the broad desk
   light
      Fills in the dreamed spaces
As the crash, the paisley shawl fallen off the piano, all the mess
   Of fallen men, black pawns
Being rolled mindlessly across the heating register
      Rattle up at me
Who, upstairs, thinking of death, find in the fuzz and purring
   And the instant of green eyes
A mental memorial that I need never really study.
      The house is cold; and fixed
In the blackness of the night outside, in the diseased old elms
      The wind can even glide
By in a silence that echoes like a final coughing, death's
      Coarse, blackening laughter,
The clatter of an idiotic cat among the chessmen.
      I know the fallen pawns
To be black from the sound of my roaring breath; and now the
   throbbing hearth
      Of unwarmed solitude
Is afire with the hoarse darkness that consumes more than flames,
      Those fitful dreams of light.

AT THE NEW YEAR

Every single instant begins another new year;
    Sunlight flashing on water, or plunging into a clearing
In quiet woods announces; the hovering gull proclaims
    Even in wide midsummer a point of turning: and fading
Late winter daylight close behind the huddled backs
    Of houses close to the edge of town flares up and shatters
As well as any screeching ram's horn can, wheel
    Unbroken, uncomprehended continuity,
Making a starting point of a moment along the way,
    Spinning the year about one day's pivot of change.
But if there is to be a high moment of turning
    When a great, autumnal page, say, takes up its curved
Flight in memory's spaces, and with a final sigh,
    As of every door in the world shutting at once, subsides
Into the bed of its fellows; if there is to be
    A time of tallying, recounting and rereading
Illuminated annals, crowded with black and white
    And here and there a capital flaring with silver and bright
Blue, then let it come at a time like this, not at winter's
    Night, when a few dead leaves crusted with frost lie shivering
On our doorsteps to be counted, or when our moments of coldness
    Rise up to chill us again. But let us say at a golden
Moment just on the edge of harvesting, "Yes. Now."
    Times of counting are times of remembering; here amidst
    showers
Of shiny fruits, both the sweet and the bitter-tasting results,
    The honey of promises gleams on apples that turn to mud
In our innermost of mouths, we can sit facing westward
    Toward imminent rich tents, telling and remembering.

Not like merchants with pursed hearts, counting in dearth and dark-
ness,
    But as when from a shining eminence, someone walking starts
At the sudden view of imperturbable blue on one hand
    And wide green fields on the other. Not at the reddening sands
Behind, nor yet at the blind gleam, ahead, of something
    Golden, looking at such a distance and in such sunlight,
Like something given—so, at this time, our counting begins,
    Whirling all its syllables into the circling wind
That plays about our faces with a force between a blow's
    And a caress', like the strength of a blessing, as we go
Quietly on with what we shall be doing, and sing
    Thanks for being enabled, again, to begin this instant.

LETTER TO JORGE LUIS BORGES:
APROPOS OF THE GOLEM

I've never been to Prague, and the last time
That I was there its stones sang in the rain;
The river dreamed them and that dream lay plain
Upon its surface, shallow and sublime.

The residues of years of dream remained
Solidified in structures on each bank;
Other dreams than of Prague and Raining sank
Under dark water as their memory waned.

And far beneath the surface of reflection
Lay a deep dream that was not Prague, but of it,
Of silent light from the gray sky above it,
The river running in some dreamed direction.

O Borges, I remember this too clearly—
Staring at paper now, having translated
Your poem of Prague, my flood of ink abated—
To have recalled it from my last trip, merely.

Three mythical cronies my great-grandfather
Was known to speak of nurture dark designs
Against my childhood: from between the lines
Of what was told me of them, I infer

How Haschele Bizensis, Chaim Pip,
The Bab Menucha and his friends, conspire
Over old pipes; sparks in a beard catch fire,
The smoke grows heavier with each slow sip . . .

I scream and wake from sleep into a room
I only remember now in dreams; my mother
Calms me with tales of Prague back in another
Time. All I remember is a tomb

Near what was called the Old-New Synagogue;
Under a baroque stone whose urn and column
Emerge in the first dawn lies, dead and solemn,
My ancestor, the Rabbi Loew of Prague.

He made The Golem (which means "embryo,"
"Potential person," much more than "machine")
Amd quickened him with a Name that has been
Hidden behind all names that one could know.

We have our family secrets: how the creature
Tried for the Rabbi's daughter, upped her dress
Till nacreous and bushy nakedness
Shone in the moonlight; groped; but failed to reach her—

How once, when heat throbbed in the August skies
And children were playing hide-and-seek, the Golem
Trailed the one who was It, and nearly stole him
Before the shadows rang with all their cries.

But was he circumcised? What glimmering rose
In his thick face at evening? Were they sham?
Did he and nine men make a quorum? I am
Not, alas, at liberty to disclose.

(But how he saved the Jews of Prague is told
In a late story—from a Polish source?—
Not to be taken seriously, of course,
No more than one about the Emperor's gold.)

These tales jostle each other in their corner
At the eye's edge, skirting the light of day
(The Bab Menucha lurks not far away,
As if around a grave, like a paid mourner).

Too dumb to live, he could not touch, but muddy:
Lest the virgin Sabbath be desecrated,
The rabbi spoke. It was deanimated;
Half-baked ceramic moldered in his study . . .

Save for the Fire of process, elements
Mix sadly: Mud is born of Water and Earth;
Air knows Water—a bubble comes to birth;
Earth and Air—nothing that makes any sense.

But bubble, mud and that incoherent third,
When animated by the Meta-Name
That is no mere breath of air itself, became
The myth whose footsteps we just overheard

Together, shuffling down a hallway, Borges,
Toward its own decreation, dull and lonely,
Lost in the meager world of one and only
One Golem, but so many Johns and Jorges.

POEM OF POOBALLS

for Reg & Naomi Pollack

Agatha shrieked as she opened the ninth door of the deal dresser;
  violet mice had been at the pooballs,
And the leaves of the ailing sycamore murmured in the wind.
For supper that night there were to have been pooballs, but the
  death of the cook necessitated a change of plan,
And we all went to Ridgely's. Jane behaved badly there, and the
  fringe of pooballs on her dress trembled
As she danced, scarcely glancing at the piano player; in between
  sets he talked to the girl with pineapple eyebrows
Who plied him with pooballs. It was a bad day all day,
And everything I did was flounder-colored. Inventions! Visions!
  It was not that you said "Why look! You've painted
Pooballs", but that the plums of sunset were unripe; night
After night I have tried to write you, for there were strange kelps
  to discuss and a table of green sea
To consider, but I am ill, hearing always the indefatigable click of
  pooballs.

But the morning yawned and expanded over the blinding water,
  searing all our mild surmises, for morning
Is a serious business. And if the remembrance of something so self-
  contained, so very like a pooball
That it rolled gurgling through the dark chasms, remained;
If resemblances to the places down which the rolling happened still
  lay in the shadows of driftwood,
There was little else for evasions to save. After the unseen waves,
  after the wailing of starlight fades, one still hears; night adheres to
These softest suggestions, cool in the sand, of something back there
  in the dark, something like something true
Of pooballs, perhaps. But yesterday's dances, yesterday's fancies,
  yesterday's glimpses

Out of the edges of the eye, of pooballs—one had wanted them
   washed unreturnably far,
Beyond regret, far past the great squint eastward, past the Capes of
   Reproach.

Now at night again. Now, the Impossibility: of pooballs; of having
   giving them room in the spheredoms, of having
Taken them at their word, the fine marbled avowals that sound like
   puffs consonant only
With contempt. The Impossibility of rolling these oily smooth un-
   broken bubbles of joke
Into endurable worlds, of plucking one last steely gleamer even
Out of the impalpable rollings, of holding it up beyond the light that
   might even now be coming from behind me,
Letting it be light. The Impossibilities of hope in Hesper's bright ball,
   bearing a last residual
Shine of night, of height. What now, then, can yet go on glimmer-
   ing, after, after this and that?
I will always go on intending to write you: of beached roses; of how
   the gray shingles of a house we looked at have caught wistaria
From the house next door; of some lost summer evening game we
   played three years ago, out there, in the late night,
With pooballs, pooballs nicking each other as I ran across the darken-
   ing lawn with a shout. I will. I will always.

COILED ALIZARINE

for Noam Chomsky

Curiously deep, the slumber of crimson thoughts:
   While breathless, in stodgy viridian,
Colorless green ideas sleep furiously.

THE POEM OF ONE LINE

A pole in air

THE WILL

from the Yiddish of Moishe Leib Halpern

Now this is how I did myself in:
No sooner did the sun begin
To shine, when I was up and away,
Gathering goat-shit for my tune
——The one I wrote just yesterday
About the moonlight and the moon——
And then I put with these also
Some poems from my portfolio
In re the bible's sanctity
(Just thinking of them sickens me)
And these I wrapped up in my rag
Of an old coat, packed up like a bag,
After which, I took the whole shebang
Put up a nail, and let it hang
Outside my window, on a tray.
Adults and children passed my way
And asked what that mess up there could be,
So I answered them, on bended knee:
These are all my years; I think
They went all rotten with infection
By wisdom, and its ancient stink,
From my precious book collection.
But when my son, the little boy,
(In my sea of sorrow and cup of joy
He's just turned four) strained his eyes to see
Those summits of sublimity,
Well——I put him on my knee
And spake thus: Harken thou to me,
My son and heir, I swear that, just
As none disturb the dead in their rest,
So, when you have finally grown,

I'll leave you thoroughly alone.
Want to be a loan-shark, a bagel-lifter?
Be one, my child.
Want to murder, set fires, or be a grifter?
Be one, my child.
Want to change off girls with the speed that those
Same girls keep changing their own clothes?
Change away, my child.
But one thing, child, I have to say:
If once ambition leads you to try
To make some kind of big display
Of yourself with what's hanging up there in the sky;
If you dare (but may that time not come soon!)
To write about moonlight and the moon,
Or some poem of the bible, poisoning the world,
Then, my dear,
If I'm worth something then by way of any
Money, so much as a single penny,
I'll make my will, leaving everything
To my *Landsman*, the future Polish King.
Though we've both stopped calling each other "thou",
I'll chop up, like a miser shredding
Cake for beggars at a wedding,
All the ties that yet bind us now.
Poppa-chopper   Son-schmon
And so   help me   God in Heaven
This
Will
Be
Done.

THE BIRD

from the Yiddish of Moishe Leib Halpern

Well, this bird comes, and under his wing is a crutch,
And he asks why I keep my door on the latch;
So I tell him that right outside the gate
Many robbers watch and wait
To get at the hidden bit of cheese,
Under my ass, behind my knees.

Then through the keyhole and the crack in the jamb
The bird bawls out he's my brother Sam,
And tells me I'll never begin to believe
How sorely he was made to grieve
On shipboard, where he had to ride
Out on deck, he says, from the other side.

So I get a whiff of what's in the air,
And leave the bird just standing there.
Meanwhile —— because one never knows,
I mean —— I'm keeping on my toes,
Further pushing my bit of cheese
Under my ass and toward my knees.

The bird bends his wing to shade his eyes
—— Just like my brother Sam —— and cries,
Through the keyhole, that *his* luck should shine
Maybe so blindingly as mine,
Because, he says, he's seen my bit
Of cheese, and he'll crack my skull for it.

It's not so nice here anymore.
So I wiggle slowly towards the door,
Holding my chair and that bit of cheese
Under my ass, behind my knees,
Quietly. But then as if I care,
I ask him whether it's cold out there.

They are frozen totally,
Both his poor ears, he answers me,
Declaring with a frightful moan
That, while he lay asleep alone
He ate up his leg —— the one he's lost.
If I let him in, I can hear the rest.

When I hear the words "ate up", you can bet
That I'm terrified; I almost forget
To guard my bit of hidden cheese
Under my ass there, behind my knees.
But I reach below and, yes, it's still here,
So I haven't the slightest thing to fear.

Then I move that we should try a bout
Of waiting, to see which first gives out,
His patience, there, behind the door,
Or mine, in my own house. And more
And more I feel it's funny, what
A lot of patience I have got.

And that's the way it's stayed, although
That was some seven years ago.
I still call out "Hi, there!" through the door.
He screams back " 'Lo, there" as before.
"Let me out" I plead, "don't be a louse"
And he answers, "Let me in the house".

But I know what he wants. So I bide
My time and let him wait outside.
He enquires about the bit of cheese
Under my ass, behind my knees;
Scared, I reach down, but, yes, it's still here.
I haven't the slightest thing to fear.

I AM

from the Yiddish of Mani Leib

I am Mani Leib, whose name is sung——
In Brownsville, Yehupetz and further, they know it;
Among cobblers, a splendid cobbler; among
Poetical circles, a splendid poet.

A boy straining over the cobbler's last
On moonlight nights . . . like a command,
Some hymn struck at my heart, and fast
The awl fell from my trembling hand.

Gracious, the first Muse came to meet
The cobbler with a kiss, and, young,
I tasted the Word that comes in a sweet
Shuddering first to the speechless tongue.

And my tongue flowed like a limpid stream,
My song rose as from some other place;
My world's doors opened onto dream;
My labor, my bread, were sweet with grace.

And all of the others, the shoemaker boys
Thought that my singing was simply grand:
For their bitter hearts, my poems were joys.
Their source? They could never understand.

For despair in their working day's vacuity
They mocked me, spat at me a good deal,
And gave me the title, in perpetuity,
Of Purple Patchmaker, Poet and Heel.

Farewell, then, Brothers, I must depart:
Your cobbler's bench is not for me.
With songs in my breast, the Muse in my heart,
I went among poets, a poet to be.

When I came, then, among their company,
Newly fledged from out my shell,
They lauded and they laurelled me,
Making me one of their number as well.

O Poets, inspired and pale, and free
As all the winged singers of the air,
We sang of Beauties wild to see
Like happy beggars at a fair.

We sang, and the echoing world resounded.
From pole to pole chained hearts were hurled,
While we gagged on hunger, our sick chests pounded:
More than one of us left this world.

And God, who feedeth even the worm——
Was not quite lavish with his grace,
So I crept back, threadbare and infirm,
To sweat my bread at my working-place.

But blessed be, Muse, for your bounties still,
Though your granaries will yield no bread——
At my bench, with a pure and lasting will,
I'll serve you solely until I am dead.

In Brownsville, Yehupetz, beyond them, even,
My name shall ever be known, O Muse.
And I'm not a cobbler who writes, thank Heaven,
But a poet, who makes shoes.

III

THE DARK MUSEUM

The dry light in this cold, usual field,
The reasonable gleam of water——no,
One awakens to these: the weariedness
Of retrieval, poverty of recollection——
The light we see in, not by which we see.

Not that green queen of silver——this is hers:
On the shores of dusk, barely-known forms come
Down to lap at the shallows shadowed deep in
Dark residual pools; and I would have drunk
Had I not hung, half in fear, behind a thicket
Like one who peers, both hands on the picture frame,
Into some of the same light that he looks out of.

Nor will your high, early lamp initiate,
O Vesperandus. Far beyond us, bluer
Than a warm bulb's ripe light, of a colder color
Than my white radiant calyx lets me pluck
Or showers across my desk: Star, hanging between
High, light-flecked peaks downtown, far yellower
Than what the icy calor of vapor streetlights
Will yet yield up. And surely I have tried
Wider lights; I have mopped at the unshown
In corners—else I had not cried out for that
Bright angel, tacked to the most hopeful blue,
That even the morning's eye, busily making
Arrangements for successional winkings, turns
Upward for, turns toward. Pale residue
Of splendor, when, rich with privileges, hushed
In a child's rounded nighttime, Moon was wont
To come as a wandering commoner, disguised
In patches of fallen radiance, as in rags
That child might scream at. Else I had not asked for

Something like this: unavailable, faint shell
Awash on a high, blue bay, or cast like a milky
Spoon of sea-glass, like the common jingle or tinkle
On a strand in shadow far below. Or like these:
Piece of the pearl; this rough, unglistening pebble
Alone remaining of those the lost children dropped;
My thumbnail pressed to the air letter that questions
"How now?" the scar of a particular, stamped
Hoofprint, struck at the summit of a wide
Loop through the clear, empty rooms of space.

Now under this white patch, even while small
Brown birds flutter at the edges of my vision
And needles of bluish fire pierce my blackness,
Something shadowless will show up, not out
Of darkness, but in this light invisible:

A puddle. An eminence of rock. In a near
Distance, some building. A path I come upon
After a crossing of scarred earth, and whose end,
At the western edge of my city's dirty garden,
The central park, I trudge toward, my shadow and I
Annihilating each other as we approach
With a clap of soundlessness that startles, as if
One heard, in the trees, the rustling of one's own wings.

TWO SLICES OF SEQUOIA

Without rooted fingers to clutch
At the underworld; resting their
Burly knuckles only against
The furred earth like some light sprinter
Waiting for a stillness to crack,
These high-crowned ones darkened the ground
Below, on which all who moved were
No more than whispering children
Running over the rust-brown rug,
Pelting each other with tiny
Cones. But here in the dark museum
Lit grayly with late city light,
The shouts of children clattering
Down long, high halls, one's mystery
Was not of tree; was not of weak
Unbelieving explorer come
Among these giants as upon
A vast dark error, a forest
Of primordial fictions. One
Wondered only what dim doors these
Great chips had been stood up against,
What half-lit corridors sealed off,
And what frightening things in glass
Cases along it kept from sight
By these immovable guardians,
Ancient but unaging now, ringed
With wisdom, and as thick as trust.

Not from the unmapped valleys of darkness, nor
The milded regions of more clouded water
   Surrounding the summits of sunken
      Mountains, the forests of shallow oceans——

But within the great flapping of foamy wings,
On the glistening feathers of spume itself,
   The astonishing, changing surf that
      Breaks on the beaches of only water,

In the thin, breathing spray flung up against the
Hot emanations of sunlight mixed unseen
   Among the gleamings, in singing air,
      Radiance, spinning at noontime, twisted

Out of the pungent methane, the dry stink of
Ammonia and generalities of
   Hydrogen, water and CO_2,
      The helical thread that we are strung on.

Was it that no generating Signal pierced
Darkening water, silencing depths, or that
   Only in those bright hurrahings of
      Accident could the rapid waves that were

Ever to flash with vision, ever to rise,
Dissolving into aspirations of their
   Own substance, carved in less than liquid,
      Returning light to the light, come to be?

Beauty as if of surface, washed up from her
Bivalve half, and half-veiled in unbridled spray,
　　Came to us from no mud-oozing depths
　　　But like someone who had always floated,

Arose, to the laughter of sunlit breakers;
Whitecaps waving farewell to the water's loss,
　　The land's new prize slipped from the roof of
　　　Ocean, onto the low Cyprian shore.

Brain coral, shelved on fringes of reef, placed in
Shallow deeps, emblems of thought bursting forth once,
　　Benign athenoma, from between
　　　Halved Olympian lobes of wisdom: sunk

To these resting places, each piece then found some
Layer of envisioning sleep below which
　　No dreaming currents of green sunlight
　　　Streamed among soft bells, making them tremble.

There are greater depths. The old mind needs only
Levels of dream to hang in where small fish streak,
　　Eyes moving rapidly, by large ones:
　　　But in what regions unsounded does this

Spiral evolve? ——singing its own enchantment:
Revolve, my line, O revolve the spinning reel,
　　Winding the curve that things grow into,
　　　Not the shrill twisting of deformation.

Depths at which this torn page of antiphonal
Or gradual music suffers its inscription
  Lie below sonorousness. This shell
    Breeds no imprisoned nymph in its chambers.

Down among the flowering choirs of shell swims
Sad, half-deaf Polyphemus, his helmeted
  Huge, plate-glass eye slowly turning as
    The length of his father's glimmering halls

Glides dimly by him. He will never find her
Here, the Nereid girl, a vanished sparkle
  Of changing wave that slides through hands in
    The sporting water, or avoids our eyes

When, from the beach recumbent, they reach over
The breaking foreground for her momentary,
  Golden flank. Even the memory
    Eludes his glassy gaze, even ghosts of

The gay, green daughters of metamorphosis
Dissolve in the sea-god's unechoing deeps.
  The diver winds his slow, watery
    Way till, lonely, he breaks the surface;

But with what bauble? High, dried, in the desk-light,
A polished bibelot, an inane snoring
  At the ear if one tries to listen:
    No whorled music survives even our heights.

A paperclip imprisons Her,
Gripping Her hidden page against
Its even one——as if a small,
Upsetting picture appearing
In my left palm were clapped away
Into the darkness of my right
One——The benign backs of the leaves
Yield only the rustle of dry
Texts: rainfall along the Nile; rice
And cotton——but no glimpses nor
Even mention of monuments.
Meanwhile, unwinkingly across
Aeons made contiguous by
Folds in a printed surface, She
Kisses Her facing page, blunted
Nose smudged away by no caress
Of Hers, as no whispering twists
The half-remembered mouth into—
A grin? A frown of leonine,
Brown, female rubble too much like
A hill? The wind of fear blew down
My slope of face and arm a month
Before, when She thrust Herself at
My unarmed eye and clung——whether
Claws sank in my consciousness or
Image, after-image adhered
Behind my awareness, claiming
All of that old kingdom. Naming
Her, that hard word that gripped the mouth
Like muscle, then vanishing in
Strangeness of x-spelled close, would hurt.

I would not look. For weeks Her stone,
Fattening on time and dry air,
Has squatted deep in sand, the parts
That will not be seen yet having
Less and less to do with legs each
Adding day. The book that hides me
From Her itself menaces now
When evening lamp shadows, cast through
A yellowed parchment shade alight
On its tall atlas spine. Four-legged
Beast, crouched on my hands and knees on
The sandstone carpet, I dare not
Reach forward toward its questions, Her
Question: What was I? What am I
To be? as reddening shadows
Fall across a desert's chilling,
Unaverted face, as a hushed
Syllable falls, unanswering——
The Mother, waiting late, disturbed——
The troublesome riddle of breath.

Generality of white light at Creation
Blindly contracted into mere orbs of yellow
   Sun and cool of moon and of icier
      Starlight. But where does it hang, the spore

Left of this narrowed blue? Midwinter wolves running
Under such final light flash signals from something
   Blue like the false ball of an eye which is
      That of no wolf, but is his who wields

Blues of the cold alone; of hurrying lateness,
Shortness of north and its furthest dark hours;
   Blue not of sky ice, but of whiteness of
      Grayness of wolf. And of other wolves

As in a rush of judgment, sudden from shadows,
Stopped, like the icy axe of a frozen comber
   Midcrested, edging some condemned, empty
      Shore. These are shadows of blue of wolves

Under the pine-broken verge the line of sky makes
With the wide, distant ice that our gaze had strained for:
   Blue not of high eyes, but of blindness of
      Failure. Of wolf. An indented line

Bares the blue light unfallen, general, coldly
Creating only itself. Pelted in thunder,
   Hard-eared, like wandering stars they skim these
      Dimmed, clouded fields, this blackness of blue.

ALASKA BROWN BEAR

O my Best Bear who stands
And, not by reason of light
But by fiat of fur, commands
The height, the essential shore, the mere,
The dryness outreaching into an icy, rich sea.

The lord of our landless pole
Is white, is white, and he hides
On stretches of chlorous ice; the pale aurora,
Rising behind him, thunders across the night.
But I am too wise now and fat
To acknowledge a lesser one, here, than His Blackness.

Teddy, the squeaky ginger,
The umptieth Marquis of Mumph,
He of the weepings: absorbent and not unfrayed
Master of childhood, midnight was in his care
In the tropic of bedroom. Then it came that I said:
I know thee not, old bear.

But He, Thou, the Big Brown, the soft turret,
Thrust by the dead earth at the sky,
Quickening yet this buff of twilight,
His she nearby——
O, downstream from Him a small
Something blurred and dark, something of baser fur
Slinks off, leaving a half-torn salmon
Before the Regent of the barest lands,
The Lord of no hall.
He stands
Among the regions of wind beyond winds. Behold!
At his own call
He has crashed through from behind the horizon
Where the great bells of summit ring with cold.

ADAM'S TASK

*"And Adam gave names to all cattle, and
to the fowl of the air, and to every
beast of the field . . ."*—Gen. 2:20

Thou, paw-paw-paw; thou, glurd; thou, spotted
    Glurd; thou, whitestap, lurching through
The high-grown brush; thou, pliant-footed,
    Implex; thou, awagabu.

Every burrower, each flier
    Came for the name he had to give:
Gay, first work, ever to be prior,
    Not yet sunk to primitive.

Thou, verdle; thou, McFleery's pomma;
    Thou; thou; thou—three types of grawl;
Thou, flisket; thou, kabasch; thou, comma-
    Eared mashawk; thou, all; thou, all.

Were, in a fire of becoming,
    Laboring to be burned away,
Then work, half-measuring, half-humming,
    Would be as serious as play.

Thou, pambler; thou, rivarn; thou, greater
    Wherret, and thou, lesser one;
Thou, sproal; thou, zant; thou, lily-eater.
    Naming's over. Day is done.

IV

THE DARKENING YARD

THE LONG AND THE SHORT OF IT

For H. Bloom, at the solar eclipse

The crescent sun, waning,
Moon-lidded, peers
Through a pinhole and lights
On a wide white card
The children hold up
In the darkening yard
At the edge of the swerving
Path of totality;
There is no wind
That could lift the hair
Of a girl who might run
In shadows too pale
To be so short;
The light has thinned,
Milked of its richness.

Fading interior
Dusk contracts
In this instant of arctic
Summer midnight
Where, silent and still
In the living room,
Two sad, fat men's
Massive bodies, hung
In the net of a moment,
Keep vigil, this shortest
Night of their lives.

They who look out of
The windows are darkened.

STOOPING FOR SALAD

In the tired yard, with soil
Far too sour for growing much
   Near the high old linden
   Dripping as in sorrow,

My shadow hangs over
The sorrel that I gather
   In the hardening
   Of the afternoon light.

MUNICH SHOWDOWN

Here in bed in this corner of
Darkened hotelroom, she who came
In pursuit of pictures sobs while
He pictures, there by the wide pane,
Pursuits of summer across royal
Green and glimpses of half-hidden
Follies among trees and cobbled
Courts shadily responding to
Their fond heels clacking. All this is
Seen piecemeal, and consumed partly
Between them: blue pictures, yellow
Palaces, silver tears. Between
Them, parting an invisible
Hard ground, a piece of night handed
Down from old partings. Lifted as
Off a platter of darkness, the
Clear dome of tomorrow will see
Them on pieced-out embassies——not
Of earth and air, not where a plane's
Vague, bland animal ascends to
A height of silver, then of speck
Of dark unrelated to the
Prostrate ground. But as, when dim cars
Start ebbing down long platforms and
Train and station terminate one
Another's lives, each receding
Part shrinks into the other's last
Picture, emptied of itself, hung
In memorial galleries,
High-ceilinged, domed and shadowing
The afternoon's descending sun.

SUNDAY A.M. NOT IN MANHATTAN

Across the street: closed shops
Where glass reflects this wide
Light only, or faintly
Etched on the sky, trolley
Lines that the overhead,
Half-open windows are
Thinking. Long, slant shadows
Cast on the wan concrete
Are of nearby fallen
Verticals not ourselves.
Lying longest, most still,
Along the unsigned blank
Of sidewalk, the narrowed
Finger of shade left by
Something, thicker than trees,
Taller than these streetlamps,
Somewhere off to the right
Perhaps, and unlike an
Intrusion of ourselves,
Unseen, long, is claiming
It all, the scene, the whole.

WHAT I SEE WHEN I LOOK UP

Where the widening sky
Over the park should have
Cut open the end of
The narrow valley whose
Enclosure I ponder,
Staring up along Sixth
Avenue; where some blue
Washes the thickening
Gray at the end of an
Afternoon; where some gray
Should have spread up from the
Street below to deaden
The bottom of the blue——

The Gizeh Sphinx, her face
The friendly, settling
Color of declining,
Warm sun, fills up the frame
Of set-back perspective
Space: as if right here,
Near the end of our way
Amongst vibrant horrors
Buzzing about, she waits,
The old familiar Fear,
Her jocund smile crumbled.
Welcoming, stony arms
Stir, under the warm sand.

GRANNY SMITH

Deep, fallen azure she flashes,
Of the grass sky beneath our feet
Untoppled yet——the greeny one,
Waiting among the usual
Fruits of our life. And why I had
Not thought to find her here among
Apples of the earth and sun, the
Bright Americans fallen or
Plucked, was: why, freshening ever
On her fable of tree, she fell
To harvest merely; why she turned
Skull-color as the dark witch dipped
Her into something bubbling; why
She dropped, green levin, to her grave
From Newton's skyward tree; why pierced
Marbles of eyes roll up in sleep,
Thin-lidded, toward the patient dark.

The aspen leaves and those of the poplars turn
Their paler faces toward the rush of the sound
Their making light of the wind releases. Bare
In her polished urn, the nymph of resonance
Whispers of breakers washing the afternoon
Sands, coppered by the declining sun; among
Her narrowing halls she drinks from the deep call
Of vowels. Sounding beside me falls the crash,
Foamy and hoarse, of this shining surface, wide
Sheets turning under themselves to splash across
Motionless limbs, hands fallen asleep in hair,
Sighing almost in silence. Below the roar
Of mingled breaths, yours ebbing against my ear,
Mine rising about the caverns that enclose
Your heart, come tidal poundings that re-emerge
From under these rustlings, this unsonorous
Reminiscence of winds that have passed among
Us, and our inarticulate leaves and shores.

HIS MASTER'S VOICE

1

Along the golden track
Of Sunday afternoon light
A triumph of motes, making
Their grave, slantward descent,
Rides down through pointed arches
And tracery, through the screen
Of stretched cloth, with a hint
Of loudspeaker's metal lip
Glistering through it. Far
Down into the radio,
They glide past shadowed regions
Where time eats light. The sound
Of Woglinde's final sighs
Dies among unseen
High, glimmering rocks, to linger
Among the bits of brightness
In the dusty caravan
Streaming in from the window.

A child plays with some chips,
Red, blue and gold on a sea
Of Chinese carpet. Hans Sachs
Hammers and sings; the lonely
English horn in a soundless
Distance hovers and lasts
In a wounded lingering.
Plangent suspensions endure,
Forever locked in the dying
Light of midafternoon.

2

Quietly snorting and rasping,
Making domestic static,
The diligent, round head
Of the faithful phonograph,
Digging a shining eyetooth
Into its homing pathway's
Unnatural, parallel spiral,
Moves toward a central cave
Of silence, where there is only
Panting of breath, the whirring
Of wide worlds turning around,
All forward motion ended.
This is the song that song
Sinks into when it dies;
Crackling of no flame, crunching
Of no particular paper,
That was and will be, whenever
Another gem, intoned
Over the oom-pah-pah thinly
Starts up, and the resonant eye
Watches us while it works.
Cave canem: "Beware:
I may sing," whispers a distant
Continuing, whirling wind.

3

Swallowed by noisy midnight,
Lamp-pierced and fraught with clamoring
Presences guarding their silence,
How many voices have darkened?
——An inaudible hiss of tape,
The whispering of revision;
A pot of green leaves falling
Against white mirroring tile.
It claims an entrance, like light.
The soprano goes into her trill.
The wind gasps for breath outside,
Making the window shake
Its mortal frame, and the slatted
Blind yield a hurried rattle,
Masking my left-handed riffle
Of pages, the scratch of my pen.

Above where larks dissolve, miles away from
Motionless piles unrocked on windy heights,
   Hard clouds approach
      Through the loud blue,

Hanging near where I ride, abandoned book
Unread, my eye wasted on the beyond
   The unsunlit
      Darkness of space,

Idle in my flying cave, mindful that
Saturn and Autumn are guilty of this:
   Emptying all
      The foreground sky,

Shrugging great wings. Inwardness hangs aloft,
Height itself towers here over the air
   Bats flutter in,
      Or brittle doves.

The sound of double-stopping, violin
Notes paired and running hand in hand
Through the hot noon sunlight, wanders over
The oatfield, high and yet unmown.

Smelling oat straw and bony, weathered wood
By the ruined barn I lie, and
Hear insistent bowings, drones, twangs, beyond
The occasional cicada,

The bird inquiring in some distant grove:
Unshaded even by the beam
Hanging amid the cloudless blue over
My head, I peer over the fields,

Over the faroff line of trees, over
The blue above them, at the high,
Gathering cumulus, summing August
Childhood, waiting for later days.

The clouds collect soundlessly. The wind at
That altitude, wailing among
White peaks, seems muffled in their melting depths.
But I will hear it later on,

Behind the underlining vapor trail
That neither connects nor divides
The rose part of the sky and the cold, blue
Region of yet-unrisen night,

But that follows a final flight eastward;
  Behind prestidigitations
Of the crippled fiddler at a spotlit
  Music festival out of doors:

The impatient panting of the high winds
  Buffetting inaccessible
Mountains of cloud whose distance from me shrinks
  Now, even as they are dissolved.

In a turning instant, my head
Catches light of a leaping star
Over my left shoulder in a
Green region of space darkened,
Into distance beyond distance,
A cold, green star, not rising like
Sons and empires, slow as breath,
In the way of stars, but as no
Darkened water could have mirrored
The partly glimpsed meteor in
Surging reversal of falling——
That sort of rising. They return
Bright rightings of our sinisters,
The mirrors; but this rise of light——
As if in summer nights at still
Moments a death could yet retract,
Or a dim candle gutter on——
Freshens the held air; far away,
Somewhere a breath has been taken.

As of an ungrounded grief,
Bluish sparks fly upward from
Under the shadow-thickened,
Tree-covered, part of night toward
What can yet be construed as
Dimmed azure, while the summer
Glow of soft streetlamp light hums
Along the wide sidewalk through
Listening leaves: fireflies
Far from the sea rise in an
Untroubled-looking midland,
Soundless, their gaps in the dark
Soundless, and the thunder soon
Coming with a crash across
Glistening eaves will be no
Answer, echo, or noisy
Amplifying of echo.
I will await what the ground,
The great, grass-skinned ground, will say.